FOCUS ON
FAMILY
MATTERS

The Effects of
Stress and Anxiety
on the Family

FOCUS ON FAMILY MATTERS

Focus on Family Matters

• • • • • • • • • • • • • •

The Effects of Stress and Anxiety on the Family

Marvin Rosen, Ph.D.

CHELSEA HOUSE
P U B L I S H E R S
A Haights Cross Communications Company
Philadelphia

CHELSEA HOUSE PUBLISHERS

EDITOR IN CHIEF Sally Cheney
DIRECTOR OF PRODUCTION Kim Shinners
CREATIVE MANAGER Takeshi Takahashi
MANUFACTURING MANAGER Diann Grasse

Staff for THE EFFECTS OF STRESS AND ANXIETY ON THE FAMILY

ASSOCIATE EDITOR Bill Conn
PICTURE RESEARCHER Sarah Bloom
PRODUCTION ASSISTANT Jaimie Winkler
COVER AND SERIES DESIGNER Takeshi Takahashi
LAYOUT 21st Century Publishing and Communications, Inc.

A Haights Cross Communications ✦ Company

http://www.chelseahouse.com

First Printing

1 3 5 7 9 8 6 4 2

Library of Congress Cataloging-in-Publication Data

Rosen, Marvin.
    The effects of stress and anxiety on the family / Marvin Rosen.
    p. cm. — (Focus on family matters)
Summary: Discusses the common causes of stress and anxiety within family
life, how to identify signs of stress, ways of coping and resources
available, and how anxiety can help to make a family stronger.
Includes bibliographical references and index.
    ISBN 0-7910-6950-8
1. Anxiety in adolescence—Juvenile literature. [1. Anxiety. 2. Stress
(Psychology) 3. Family problems.] I. Title. II. Series.
BF724.3.A57 R67 2002
152.4'6—dc21   2002005769

Contents

Introduction

Marvin Rosen, Ph.D.
Consulting Editor

B ad things sometimes happen to good people. We've probably all heard that expression. But what happens when the "good people" are teenagers?

Growing up is stressful and difficult to negotiate. Teenagers are struggling to becoming independent, trying to cut ties with their families that they see as restrictive, burdensome, and unfair. Rather than attempting to connect in new ways with their parents, they may withdraw. When bad things do happen, this separation may make the teen feel alone in coping with difficult and stressful issues.

Focus on Family Matters provides teens with practical information about how to cope when bad things happen to them. The series deals foremost with feelings—the emotional pain associated with adversity. Grieving, fear, anger, stress, guilt, and sadness are addressed head on. Teens will gain valuable insight and advice about dealing with their feelings, and for seeking help when they cannot help themselves.

The authors in this series identify some of the more serious problems teens face. In so doing, they make three assumptions: First, teens who find themselves in difficult situations are not at fault and should not blame themselves. Second, teens can overcome difficult situations, but may need help to do so. Third, teens bond with their families, and the strength of this bond influences their ability to handle difficult situations.

These books are also about communication—specifically about the value of communication. None of the problems covered occurs in a vacuum, and none of the situations should be faced by anyone alone. Each either involves a close family member or affects the entire family. Since families teach teens how to trust, relate to others, and solve problems, teens need to bond with families to develop normally and become emotionally whole. Success in dealing with adversity depends not only on the strength of the individual teen, but also upon the resources of the family in providing support, advice, and material assistance. Strong attachment to care givers in a supporting, nurturing, safe family structure is essential to successful coping.

Some teens learn to cope with adversity—they absorb the pain, they adjust, and they go on. But for others, the trauma they experience seems like an insurmountable challenge—they become angry, stressed, and depressed. They may withdraw from friends, they may stop going to school, and their grades may slip. They may draw negative attention to themselves and express their pain and fear by rebelling. Yet, in each case, healing can occur.

The teens who cope well with adversity, who are able to put the past behind them and regain their momentum, are no less sensitive or caring than those who suffer most. Yet there is a difference. Teens who are more resilient to trauma are able to dig deep down into their own resources, to find strength in their families and in their own skills, accomplishments, goals, aspirations, and values. They are able to find reasons for optimism and to feel confidence in their capabilities. This series recognizes the effectiveness of these strategies, and presents problem-solving skills that every teen can use.

Focus on Family Matters is positive, optimistic, and supportive. It gives teens hope and reinforces the power of their own efforts to handle adversity. And most importantly, it shows teens that while they cannot undo the bad things that have happen, they have the power to shape their own futures and flourish as healthy, productive adults.

What is Anxiety?

Michael feels anxious and afraid almost all the time. Although he is a good student and the captain of the football team, he has trouble sleeping and has bouts of nausea. Most of his family and friends would be surprised to learn that beneath his confident exterior, he is bundle of nerves.

Michael was in New York City on September 11, 2001, the day that the World Trade Center was destroyed by terrorists. He and his friends had been at a museum in another part of the city, but they could see the smoke in the distance. Ever since then, Michael has been worried and can't concentrate in school. He spends his days—and nights—waiting for something terrible to happen.

We live in a time when anxiety is common. We are concerned about terrorist attacks, and flying in airplanes. We are anxious about anthrax and other biological weapons. We are uncertain about what the future holds. We do not always feel safe in our schools. The world can seem like a dangerous place.

In today's world, it is often difficult to feel safe, even when no clear danger exists. Even the routine pressures of our daily schedules can make us feel like we're always one step behind.

This feeling is not unique to Americans. In many parts of the world where war, hunger, and violence are common, each day can bring new dangers. Nor is this feeling new. In the 1950s, shortly after World War II ended, the poet W. H. Auden described that period of time as "the age of anxiety."

The news is often filled with stories that can increase your anxiety. Reports of school shootings, unexpected airline disasters and horrible car accidents can leave you wondering if you are truly safe anywhere. The future can seem as if it is full of question marks. News of a major attack or attempted attack on the U.S.—

like the September 11, 2001 terrorist attacks—can leave you struggling with feelings of fear, frightening dreams, difficulty concentrating, trouble sleeping, and even feelings of anger or other intense emotions.

Stress in the wild

A gray squirrel encounters a wolf in the forest. The wolf prepares to attack. The squirrel spies a tree about 20 yards away and makes a dash for it, reaching the safety of the tree before the wolf can pounce.

This simple story is a regular part of life in the wild. But the responses from the animals are far from simple. Their reactions took place because of a complex set of biological, emotional, and psychological signals. Both predator (the wolf) and potential victim (the squirrel) had to recognize the situation, and what they recognized was quite different. The squirrel understood the danger; the wolf understood the opportunity to attack. That recognition, involving the processing of information from several senses, caused a response from both the body and the emotions. The squirrel, aware that it was no match for the wolf, felt fear and ran for safety. The wolf, recognizing a meal and aware of its own physical superiority, gave chase. Biologists label this set of impulses as the **fight or flight reaction**.

The fight or flight reaction refers to the animal's natural ability to assemble the physical resources required for survival. The animal will either stand and fight or attempt to escape. Human beings also have such resources. They are aroused in times of crisis or in an emergency. We commonly see them in soldiers dealing with battle conditions. In

Can you describe how the fight or flight reaction helps an animal survive in the wild?

both humans and animals, these are survival mechanisms. They provide more energy and strength, help us think clearly, help us to cope with stressful situations. Humans, of course, take these skills one step higher, by adding the ability to solve problems and plan ahead. But the basic fight or flight skills stay with us, becoming available if needed.

This survival mechanism in humans can sometimes go wrong. In many people, attempting to cope with the stresses and pressures of modern society, it appears to work overtime. It fails to shut off. They respond as if every condition was an immediate emergency. They are constantly on their guard, ever vigilant, expecting the worst, worrying about consequences and imagined future disasters. They experience fear, yet often it is unclear exactly what is upsetting them. Rather than a specific event, they feel a vague, general sense of worry. This condition is known as **anxiety**. Anxiety has three parts—a physical reaction affecting many organs and biological systems; a feeling of worry or dread; and a set of behaviors and symptoms that vary in different persons. Let's examine these reactions in more detail.

When a person interprets a situation as being dangerous, a series of events occur in the body to mobilize the body's resources. The adrenal gland secretes a chemical substance called **adrenalin** that enters the blood stream, travels through the body, and triggers a series of reactions. The blood vessels of the skin contract so that blood is forced to the muscles and brain. (This is why a person who is frightened looks pale.) They may shiver or pant, or breathe more deeply or more quickly. Next, the liver secretes a sugar to the muscles for more energy. The fear is clear in a frightened person's eyes: their pupils dilate and their eyes become wide. Their heart beats more rapidly to send more blood to the brain and the muscles. They may begin to sweat—the body's way of cooling itself off in preparation for action. Muscles become tense. These are all the body's way of preparing itself for the emergency.

Anxiety is common—we all feel it at different times for different reasons. The outside situation—the event or person that has made you feel anxious—is called the **stressor**. Your stressor may be a frightening teacher, an exam scheduled for next week, or an illness in a family member. It is interesting that no one stressor causes the same reaction in everyone. You may be worried about Friday's quiz while your friends are not. One teacher may make you feel anxious and uncomfortable, while others in the class react differently.

What is the difference between stress and a stressor?

A little bit of anxiety can actually improve performance. It may help you (or force you) to do something that needs to be done, like studying for an exam or finishing your chores. It is when anxiety becomes more intense that it can interfere with your life—and your thinking. A good example is test anxiety. Some students just cannot handle the stress of tests. They study hard the night before. They seem to know the material. Yet during the exam their mind goes blank. All they can seem to think of are the consequences of failing. They start to shake or to sweat. The exam begins to feel like an overwhelming situation that they can't handle. Their anxiety becomes so great that it turns into panic.

In addition to interfering with your ability to function in particular situations (during a test, in a particular teacher's classroom), chronic anxiety has long-term consequences. High anxiety levels can be dangerous to your health. We are given a limited number of physical skills and resources to deal with emergencies. These skills and resources can be

When our normal survival mechanisms go wrong, we can find ourselves overwhelmed by feelings of fear or dread. Such anxiety can affect our concentration and our performance at school. "Blanking out" during an exam is one effect of anxiety.

used up, leaving your body less able to cope with stresses and physical problems. Constant high levels of anxiety can trigger heart problems, ulcers, headaches, and skin reactions. It can reduce your immune system that fights infection and disease, making you more likely to become sick. There are even some links that have been shown to connect anxiety with cancer. If you spend a lot of your time feeling anxious (and many people do), it is important to do something about it.

How it happens

For many years, biologists and psychologists have been investigating what makes people anxious and how they learn to respond the way they do. The answers to these questions can provide clues about effective treatments. Did you ever step off the curb on a busy street and then quickly step back as a car or truck rushes by? Safely back on the sidewalk, you feel a wave of fear overwhelm you. "I might have been killed," you think. Why is it that you feel fear at that point—after the incident is over and you are safe?

A well-known psychologist named William James believed that emotion is the awareness of our body's reactions. Imagine that you have gone into a forest and seen a bear. You run away, feel yourself running and feel your heart beating. Then you feel afraid. James believed that it was you realizing that your body was running and that your heart was beating fast that made you feel fear. That theory was popular for a while but it ignored one thing—the brain. Today, we understand that we experience emotions because of the way we process information about the events happening around us plus our body's response to them.

A well-known study of college students by psychologists Stanley Schachter and Jerome Singer shows just how this works. In the experiment, the students volunteered to participate in the research, but were not told what was being studied. One-half of the students were given shots of adrenalin (the substance that our body secretes to signal danger). The other half was also given shots, but of a **placebo** (a substance that has no physical effects). The two groups were then again divided. Some of the students (without the others knowing) were directed to act in a certain way when they were back with the others—to pretend to be annoyed and impatient about how long it was taking for the experiment to begin. In a second group, certain students were instructed to "lighten up the mood." When they went back to the rest of the students, they made jokes and laughed.

Psychologist William James (seen here in 1911) studied people's emotional reactions in an attempt to understand the causes of anxiety. Although his theories have been replaced by more modern ideas, he laid some important groundwork in our understanding of emotional stress.

All of the students were then asked to perform some task—something that was completely unrelated to the point of the research. This was done just to disguise the true focus of the study. Before leaving, the students were interviewed and asked about any feelings they might have had during the investigation.

The results are very interesting. The students who had been given the placebo reported no special feelings, no matter what the other students in the room with them did. But the students who had been given shots of adrenalin were much more likely to say that they had some sort of emotional reaction to what was going on around them. If they were in the group with the irritated student, they said that they were really angry at having had to wait. If they were in the group with the joking student, they reported feeling happy and having had a great time.

The results from this study help us to understand how emotions work in general and how we experience anxiety. First, there must be some physical factor or trigger. The shots of adrenalin in the study provided this "trigger." Next, there should be some clues from the people around us or the setting in which we find ourselves to help us interpret why our body is reacting the way it is. In the study of the college students, these clues were provided by the student "planted" in the room and given a specific behavior to act out.

It is interesting to realize that different emotions do not spark different physical responses. The same basic set of physical responses is used for all intense emotions. It is up to us to figure out why we are having the reaction we are having, based on what is going on and around us. If we decide that something bad is happening, we may feel concerned or worried—a feeling we recognize as tension or anxiety. Knowing that these two things have to happen—a physical response and our own interpretation of it—shows how anxiety can be treated. Treatment can focus on either the triggering of the physical response, or the way

How do you feel when you are angry, excited, or very happy? Are your physical responses different for each of these emotions?

in which we process it. In Chapter 5, we will discuss these approaches to treatment in more detail.

Anxiety and performance

In small doses, anxiety can help motivate you. If your teacher announces that there will be a social studies test next week, you may begin to feel slightly anxious. But you don't do anything about it for several days. As the day of the test gets closer, you feel more and more anxiety. Finally, you can't take it anymore! You sit down and begin to study. This is how you manage your anxiety—you begin to study in order to reassure yourself that you will be able to handle the test.

This same kind of motivation can work in sports. Many athletes say that they perform better when they feel slightly anxious during an event.

But a little anxiety goes a long way. Small amounts of anxiety can encourage you to work harder. But excessive anxiety can make it nearly impossible to function.

Focusing on the family

As we learned in the study of college students, anxiety can be increased by the behavior of other people. For this reason, many therapists prefer to include the whole family when helping teens overcome anxiety. Their belief is that the actions of some family members can contribute to, or lessen, feelings of anxiety in others in the family. If one family member is experiencing anxiety, there may be problems in the rest of the family that need to be addressed as part of the treatment. The ways in which anxiety affects family functioning, as well as family approaches to treatment, will be explored in Chapter 6.

What Causes Anxiety?

■ "I set my alarm, but I usually sleep right through it. My mom leaves for work early, so she can't wake me up. I feel like I'm always rushing. I never have time for breakfast. I have to run to the corner every morning to catch the bus. Sometimes I'm in such a hurry that I forget my homework or my books. There's always something missing. The teachers get mad if I forget stuff for school, my mom gets mad if I forget something at home. It feels like I always have someone mad at me. My stomach hurts all the time. I guess it's stress."

–Joe, 7th grade.

The nervous system

In order to understand how anxiety causes physical and biological changes, you first need to understand a little about the structure and function of the nervous system. The nervous system has two main parts. The first part, or system, is known as the **somatic nervous system**. This controls the working of

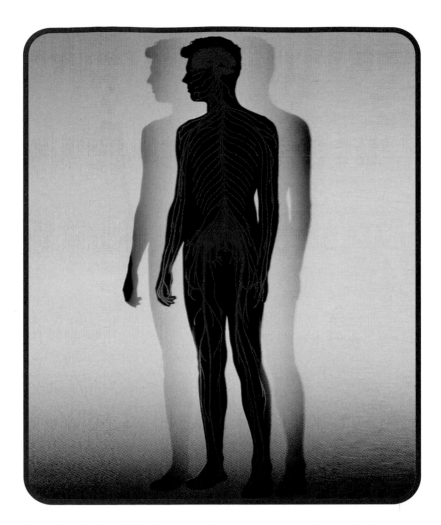

The physical and biological changes we experience during periods of anxiety or stress can be traced to the central nervous system. Two important sub-systems of the autonomic nervous system—the parasympathetic and sympathetic nervous systems—link our perceptions to involuntary responses in our bodies.

your voluntary muscles. It controls the inputs from your various sense organs and the responses of your muscles.

There is another part of the nervous system, called the **autonomic nervous system**. This is a system that you may not be aware of—unless it goes wrong. The autonomic nervous system is itself divided into two parts. The first part, the **parasympathetic nervous system**, controls the muscles of your glands and internal organs. It controls the process by which you digest food, for example. The other part of the autonomic nervous system controls some of the physical responses we've discussed earlier—things like your startle reaction and your fight or flight response. It is called the **sympathetic nervous system**. This is the system that causes emotional changes to occur in your body. It releases adrenalin into the blood, speeds up your heart rate, and in many other ways prepares your body to deal with danger. How does it work? There are certain outside factors—things like loud noises, for example—that may cause a physical response by sending a message to the lower parts of your brain. But some signals connect to the higher parts of your brain, like the cerebral cortex. The cerebral cortex is the part of your brain that interprets outside conditions as dangerous and also may trigger some physical response. The cerebral cortex has access to memories of past experiences, and may make a connection between something relatively harmless and some earlier event. This is why some people experience sudden anxiety in a place or under certain conditions that, to us, seem very normal and not at all dangerous.

Can you describe the role each part of the central nervous system plays in creating anxiety?

These two systems—the sympathetic and parasympathetic nervous systems—work in balance with each other. They interact like the brake and gas pedal of a car to keep the body working smoothly. When something goes wrong with these systems, the body will respond in unexpected ways.

Some people may have a biological predisposition to anxiety—that means that something about their physical or genetic makeup makes it more likely that certain events and situations will make them anxious. It as if their sympathetic nervous system is more easily "switched on." For other people, who tend to be more laid back, the parasympathetic system may be more easily "switched on."

What role does psychology play?

Studies have shown that there are certain environmental conditions that appear to make people more anxious and spark anxious behavior. To help clarify which conditions or situations will tend to make people more anxious, researchers first study animals to determine which factors make the most difference in creating anxiety. One important type of situation related to anxiety is called **conflict**. In research experiments, conflict can occur when a goal has both pluses and minuses. Suppose that an animal must cross an electrified grid to get to its food box. The closer he comes to the food and the shock, the more the conflict and the higher the anxiety.

What about for us? Where does conflict spark anxiety in people? Perhaps you've been offered a part-time job after school, but you already have track practice scheduled at the same time. Trying to make the choice—job or sports—may make you anxious. Conflict can also be created when you have to choose between two equally good options. Perhaps you've made two different sports teams, but they both

What is a conflict and how does it create anxiety?

practice at the same time. Which one do you choose? The choice can create anxiety. Usually, this type of conflict doesn't last long. As soon as you make the choice and start moving in that direction, your choice will seem better and better. The closer you get to your goal, the better it will seem to you.

Another source of anxiety comes from your sense of

control over your future. How much control you believe you can have over future events is one of the most important factors in whether or not you experience stress. Stress has the best chance of attacking you when you feel the most helpless. An utter sense of helplessness can lead to terrible results—even death.

We can look to the cases of prisoners held in concentration camps during World War II for an example. The prisoners held under horrible conditions suffered terrible mistreatment. Millions were killed in gas chambers. Those who survived reported two types of reactions. Some continued to believe that they would survive and found ways to stay positive. Others, believing there was nothing they could do to save themselves, gave up and became what the prisoners called "zombies," existing in a kind of living death.

In a similar way, studies of elderly residents of nursing homes show that those who believe they have personal control of their daily lives are happier, more active, and more alert than those who feel helpless and dependent on their care givers. Similar cases are reported in hospitals—patients who feel in control of their situation experience less stress, even with painful procedures, get better faster, and have shorter hospital stays.

So, where does anxiety get started? One way of looking at it is to think of anxiety as a breakdown in your psychological defenses. Sigmund Freud, who pioneered many of the modern approaches to treating mental disorders, focuses on this "defense system." In studying patients with anxiety, Freud recognized that their personality reacted defensively when it became aware of danger or threatening thoughts. This system of protection against anxiety depended on certain strategies, which we call **defense mechanisms**. Freud believed that these mechanisms were unconscious and that they always involved a certain degree of distorting reality.

Persistent feelings of helplessness can dramatically increase our anxiety. Studies of elderly nursing home residents have shown that those who experience a greater control over their daily lives tend to be happier than those who feel dependent on their caregivers.

One of these defense mechanisms is called repression—the dangerous or frightening thought is pushed back out of your mind. Seems like a good system, right? But it never works completely—the frightening or dangerous thought often pops up in dreams, slips of the tongue, or other behaviors that you can't control.

Another defense mechanism is regression. In regression, you attempt to step back in time by acting and behaving as if you were much younger. Young children may suddenly want to be carried everywhere, for example, and older children or adults may show a similar need for situations that feel comforting. You may want to spend more time in bed, for instance, because it suddenly feels safe.

Reaction formation is a defense in which you act in a way that is opposite to the way you really feel. You may overcome your fears by acting brave or doing something courageous. You may convince yourself that you really like someone with whom you are very angry.

Yet another defense mechanism is projection. In projection, you place your own fears or unacceptable emotions on someone else. You may be feeling very angry with someone, but feel that acting out on that angry feeling could be dangerous, so instead you become convinced that that person is angry with you.

Rationalization is another defense. This is when you come up with an explanation for doing something rather than admitting the real reason why you are behaving in a particular way. You may tell yourself, "There's no point to studying for that test, because the teacher hates me," and so you watch television rather than opening the book.

What is a defense mechanism

and is it a healthy response to anxiety?

Displacement is when you take a strong feeling that you have for one person—a feeling that you cannot safely express to that person—and instead put it on someone else. A parent may be criticized by his or her boss and then come home and yell at their children, not because they are really angry with the children but because they cannot safely express their anger at their boss (without losing their job!).

Finally, there is sublimation. In sublimation, unacceptable behavior is transformed into acceptable behavior. How? Strong feelings—things like aggression or anger—can be transformed into competitive behavior in sports. A defensive tackle on the football team may take his anger (anger sparked by a problem at school) and use it to push himself harder during practice and football games.

These mechanisms can all be sparked by anxiety. Your mind can be using these different defense mechanisms without you even being aware of it.

Emotional support from family members is an important tool in overcoming anxiety. Studies have shown that when more than two generations of a single family live together, individual family members experience fewer health problems.

Focusing on the family

Most people have developed effective support systems to help get past the bumps in life. If you are lucky enough to have a loving family, you get comfort from the knowledge that they are there for you if you need them. Friends and relatives can also give us this sense of support and security.

When support systems fail, for whatever reason, you are more likely to experience anxiety. Family structures make a difference. Studies have shown that when extended families (more than two generations) are living together, the family members experience fewer health problems.

The importance of the ways in which family members communicate and support each other are explored more in the last chapter of this book.

Suffering from Anxiety

■ Billy was 13 when he stopped going to school, shortly after his parents' divorce. Always a nervous child, he learned to fear social situations. He often had stomachaches on school days. Billy's mom worried about his health. If he complained of stomachaches, she kept him home from school. He had a particularly tough teacher in middle school, and his stomachaches became more frequent. He missed more and more school. The school principal became suspicious that Billy really wasn't sick. She believed that he had developed a school phobia and that it would get worse if he wasn't helped. Instead of following his suggestion that Billy get professional help, Billy's mom became angry with the principal for being unsympathetic to his medical problems. Billy continued to miss school.

Now that we understand how the sympathetic and parasympathetic nervous systems work, we can begin to examine the role that the mind plays in triggering these reactions.

Severe fears (or phobias) can cause people to avoid certain people, places, or things. A student with social phobia, for example, might distance himself from other kids at school because he fears what they might say or do to him.

Psychologists have long been interested in the ways in which psychological processes can affect the functioning of the body. Ancient Greek philosophers even had a name for this question—they called it the "the mind-body problem." There are still many questions about exactly how the mind and body interact, but there is little doubt that mental processes interact with bodily organs in many ways.

These interactions affect your health.

Some anthropologists have discovered evidence that, in certain cultures, thoughts and beliefs could trigger such extreme body reactions that they would actually lead to death. How is this possible? In certain remote, primitive cultures, someone would do something so extreme that the society would decide that they could no longer stay in the community. The community would shun this person—in essence, they would behave as if the person was dead. The entire community would react as if the person had died. The experience of being a social outcast—of being treated as if he or she had died—would be so overwhelmingly upsetting that, in some cases, the person actually would die. This phenomenon, also known as bone pointing or voodoo death, depended on the actions and beliefs of not only one person, but the entire community as well.

The possibility that extreme fear, by activating the sympathetic nervous system, can cause death is real and the source of the popular expression "scared to death." Extreme fear or frequent anxiety can produce changes in the function of many bodily organs in ways we identify as disease. Excessive production of sugar because of fear can produce the symptoms of diabetes, for example. High stress can bring on or increase your risk for heart disease and high blood pressure. Anxiety can make you "sick to your stomach"—causing such stomach problems as peptic ulcers and spastic colon. Some studies have even shown that anxiety can contribute to such conditions as asthma or migraine headaches.

What is the connection

between your mind and your body? Can anxiety make you sick?

More recent research has found links between anxiety and your immune system. It appears that anxiety can reduce your resistance to germs. Some reports suggest that even life-threatening illness such as cancer may be linked to anxiety. Of course, anxiety alone does not cause these diseases. Genetics plays an important role. People may inherit a predisposition toward certain diseases. Your diet, the amount that you exercise, and your lifestyle also contribute to your resistance to disease. But research has shown that there is a relationship between your physical and mental health.

Psychological effects

While certain behaviors seem to be the result of anxiety, these behaviors could also cause you to become anxious (in part because of the reactions from others to these behaviors).

The psychological (or mental) consequences of anxiety can be divided into two categories. The first are behaviors and personality patterns that seem to be driven by anxiety. These may be behaviors that make certain reactions more likely, or they may be behaviors that help you avoid certain reactions. The second category relates to the breakdown of your psychological defenses. These are ways that you have consciously or unconsciously learned to avoid anxiety or reduce it. These may be mild, more like a kind of personality style (like being a "take-charge" person, or someone who doesn't go to parties), or they may be more serious and result in a condition severe enough to be described as an emotional problem or anxiety disorder.

Certain types of personalities have been shown to place you at higher risk for health problems like heart attacks. One of these is described as a "Type A personality." A Type A personality is someone who is very aggressive about reaching their goals; behaves as if they are constantly under pressure; and is extremely competitive and focuses on achieving things. You can see that anxiety can play a role in shaping this kind of behavior.

Psychiatrists and psychologists have recognized certain personality disorders that are related to anxiety. A personality disorder is a set of unusual or abnormal behaviors— behaviors that generally begin when you are a teen or young adult and continue over a period of time. One such personality disorder is called Avoidant Personality. Teens with this disorder avoid school or other activities out of fear of disapproval, rejection, or criticism. They are shy, timid, quiet, easily embarrassed, and insecure.

Can you describe how a personality disorder may be both the result of anxiety, and the cause of more anxiety?

When criticized, they may blush or even cry. They avoid making friends unless they are certain that the person will be completely accepting of them.

A Dependent Personality refers to a person who has a need to be taken care of and protected. When you have a dependent personality, you cling to people and find it difficult to make any decisions or do anything on your own. You lack self-confidence and worry about making other people angry. You avoid disagreeing with other people or expressing your own opinion, simply because you don't want to make the other person angry.

An Obsessive-Compulsive Personality is someone who is totally focused on things being in their proper place, on being clean, on being on time, on being perfect. If you have an obsessive-compulsive personality, you will avoid anxiety by attempting to control situations and by obeying the rules,

A personality disorder may place you at a higher risk for developing anxiety. Therapists can recognize these disorders, and help you adapt strategies that will reduce your risk of developing anxiety-related problems.

paying attention to even the smallest details, making lists and schedules. You also will tend to hoard things—magazines, newspapers, and old clothes—because you may someday need them. You cannot stand mistakes—either your own or other people's. You want things done your way and no other. You are stubborn, you don't like to admit that anyone else can be right, and you often don't like to spend money. This behavior is a way of keeping control and so reducing stress, but the result is a personality who can be too controlling of themselves and other people, wasting time and energy in their effort to manage every detail.

These personality types may sound familiar to you—perhaps you recognize some of your own traits, or someone else's. These personality types are all around us. While some of their behaviors can be irritating or annoying to other people, these behaviors seem normal to them. They usually do not seek or require treatment because their defenses against anxiety work for them very well.

The most extreme expressions of anxiety occur in conditions known as anxiety disorders. In these cases, anxiety or the symptoms related to anxiety interfere with daily living and usually require outside help, such as therapy and/or medication.

Phobias (fears) are one example of this kind of anxiety disorder. A phobia is a severe form of anxiety, coming from a particular object or situation. For example, some people have a fear of heights, or snakes, or flying, or small, enclosed places. People who suffer from phobias generally do their best to avoid whatever it is that makes them anxious. One extreme (and fairly common) phobia is agoraphobia. If you suffer from agoraphobia, you are afraid of getting into a situation from which you may not be able to get help or escape. Some agoraphobics are unable to leave the safety of their homes without experiencing severe anxiety. It may involve fear of being in crowds, traveling in an automobile or subway, crossing a bridge, or entering a large department store. Another common phobia is social phobia. This is a type of anxiety caused by certain types of social situations. One 13-year-old boy who suffered from social phobia could not walk past small groups of students in school. He typically waited until the last minute to leave for school to avoid feeling uncomfortable waiting for school to start.

Certain types of anxiety disorders are much less specific.

Severe anxiety can cause us to withdraw from life in many ways. Someone with a phobia of flying, for example, may avoid a potentially fun or profitable trip because of her fear of airplanes.

Generalized anxiety disorder refers to anxiety related to a wide range of situations—you feel worried and anxious all of the time. You may feel restless, exhausted and tense, and find it difficult to concentrate or to sleep.

Post-traumatic stress disorder occurs after one or more traumatic experiences, such as an attack, a car accident, or a natural disaster like an earthquake or tornado. When you suffer from post-traumatic stress disorder, you are constantly suffering from nightmares or thoughts about what happened, and constantly trying to avoid situations that remind you of what happened. You never feel truly safe.

We discussed obsessive-compulsive personality earlier. In its more extreme form, known as obsessive-compulsive disorder, you experience many of the traits we talked about earlier, but in addition you suffer from constant worrying thoughts (obsessions) and feel a need to repeat certain rituals or routines. You may feel the need to keep going back to check that you locked the front door, or find it difficult to handle a bathroom doorknob or money because you are so worried about germs.

Panic disorder is another extreme symptom of anxiety. If you suffer from panic disorder, you feel out of control. You feel such intense panic that you believe you may be going crazy, having a heart attack or even dying. You may believe that there is something serious wrong with you—perhaps that you have some life-threatening disease that the doctors have not yet discovered.

Social effects

A talented young singer is offered an opportunity to participate in a national vocal competition. She will be given the chance to compete for a cash prize and a scholarship to a nationally famous music school. It is a tremendous opportunity, but the competition is being held in a different part of the country from where she lives, and she will have to fly there. She has only taken one other airplane trip, and it was a terrible experience. She completely panicked, disrupting the flight and embarrassing herself and her family. She has vowed never again to get on a plane, and the thought of traveling in one now leaves her feeling such intense fear that she knows that she will need to give

What would you do

if you were offered a once-in-a-lifetime opportunity, but felt too anxious to pursue it?

up her place in the competition. There is no way that she will ever get on a plane after what happened the last time.

Anxiety can be crippling in many ways. Anxiety can cause emotional chaos, but it also affects how you interact with other people. It can make you avoid certain situations, simply because you are afraid. It can make you shy, withdrawn, unwilling to take risks. And what if anxiety makes you afraid of criticism, or failure, or rejection? Success only happens when you are willing to take chances and risks. If you back away from challenges, if you fail to stand up for yourself, if you are willing to settle for less, your world will become smaller and bleaker. Safe perhaps, but also very boring.

Measuring Anxiety

■ "I've just got to learn to deal with the stress that I'm feeling. I toss and turn every night. I keep thinking about what I have to do the next day. I'm tired every morning and I can barely drag myself out of bed to get to school on time. When I do get up, I'm just a basket case. I know I'm not getting the sleep I need. I seem to worry about everything but when I have a test to deal with it just blows me away. I try to study and I know I understand the material but when the test papers are handed out, I keep thinking of what will happen if I fail instead of concentrating on the questions. I can feel my heart racing and sometimes I can't catch my breath. My parents are on my case all the time. They can't understand why I get such bad grades."

–Kim, 8th grade.

In Chapter 1, you learned that there are three parts to anxiety—feelings, body reactions, and behaviors. All three of these reactions can be measured in order to determine just

There are several ways to measure anxiety. By examining our feelings, physical reactions, and behaviors, we can get a better picture of the way anxiety affects our lives.

how anxious you may be. The last two are the easiest, although specialized equipment may be necessary. Physical reactions can be determined indirectly by looking for biological symptoms of anxiety, such as how often you get a stomachache. It can be measured more directly by sophisticated measures of muscle activity, skin resistance, heart rate, blood pressure, breathing, etc. Behaviors such as avoiding or withdrawing from situations can also be counted and calculated. Feelings are, of course, more difficult to measure. But it can be done by interviews, special rating scales, and psychological testing. Another approach is to count the number of stressful events (stressors) a person has to deal with and assume that the more of these events you have, the more stress you will feel (although it does not account for the fact that different people deal with stress differently).

Age matters

It seems obvious, but it is important to remember that at different ages, we worry about different things. Babies worry only about feeling safe and getting their needs met. Preschoolers worry about monsters, witches, and other scary things. As you get older, your circle of worry expands to include your parents and family members. When you are in school, you worry about teachers, tests, and being teased. Pre-teens become self-conscious and need to be accepted for their clothing and their behavior. As you get older, you begin to add to the list of worries, with things like cliques, gangs, drugs, peer pressure, dating, and trying to figure out exactly who you are and what you want to become.

How is age related to the types of things you worry about?

See if you can find any of your own worries on the list below:

- Failing a test at school
- My parents being disappointed in me
- My parents getting divorced
- Not being popular
- Speaking before a group in school
- Not being a success
- Being poor
- Violence in my neighborhood
- Pressure to do drugs
- Sickness of a parent
- Death of a parent
- Death of a friend
- Not being attractive
- Acts of terrorism
- Friends not sticking by me
- Biological warfare

Test anxiety is common among students. When fears of failure become overwhelming, they can interfere with your ability to perform well in school. Interfering thoughts can make you "blank out" during a test and can reduce self-confidence about future exams.

Test anxiety

Anxiety comes in many forms. Sometimes it is general—a vague, anxious feeling that something, somehow is wrong. Sometimes it is specific—there is a clear reason why you are feeling worried. One common source of anxiety can be the experience of taking a test. If you have ever experienced test anxiety, you may have found yourself thinking some of the following thoughts: "I can't pass this test." "I am stupid. " "If I fail this test, terrible things will happen." "Everyone will know what an idiot I am. " These type of thoughts are called

interfering thoughts—they literally *interfere* with your ability to perform in a specific situation. Interfering thoughts probably occur because you have had bad experiences with tests before. You have learned on such occasions that you will not do well. Wherever they come from, interfering thoughts will make it impossible for you to concentrate and do well, even when you know the material! Does this apply to you?

There are scales that measure test anxiety. They contain true or false items such as those below:

1. When I have to take a math test I spend a lot of time worrying about it. True _____ False _____

2. When I take a test I feel myself becoming very emotional. True _____ False _____

3. When I take a test I worry about failing—not just failing the test, but failing all of my classes.
   True _____ False _____

4. I can't stand waiting for my teacher to pass back my graded exam. True _____ False _____

5. I wish I only had to take classes that gave take-home exams. True _____ False _____

The more times that you answered "True" to the questions above, the more likely it is that you have experienced test anxiety at one time or another.

General anxiety

In addition to measuring test anxiety, other tests have been designed to measure more general anxiety. Some of the questions you might find on these tests would be the following:

1. I have headaches frequently. True _____ False _____

2. When I am upset, my stomach churns.
   True _____ False _____

3. I always seem to be worrying about something.
   True _____ False _____

4. My problems seem to pile up so high that I feel I cannot deal with them. True _____ False _____

5. My thoughts keep racing so badly that I cannot concentrate in school. True _____ False _____

6. I'm always worrying about grades. True _____ False _____

7. I have no self-confidence. True _____ False _____

8. Whenever there is a challenge, I feel that I will fail.
   True _____ False _____

Life Stressors Checklists

Another way to measure anxiety is by counting up the number of stressful life events that you are currently experiencing. While everyone experiences stress differently, it is generally true that the more stressful life events you are experiencing, the greater will be your anxiety. Your stress checklist might include the following:

1. I have recently experienced the death of a close family member. True _____ False _____

2. My parents recently separated or divorced.
   True _____ False _____

3. I was recently injured or suffered an illness.
   True _____ False _____

4. A close member of my family is sick.
   True _____ False _____

5. I am having relationship problems with my boyfriend or girlfriend. True _____ False _____

6. I have a new stepparent. True _____ False _____

7. My parents have had a new baby. True _____ False _____

8. I recently experienced the death of a close friend.
    True _____ False _____

9. I have recently moved. True _____ False _____

10. I have recently changed schools. True _____ False _____

Biological measurement

Other measures of anxiety measure physical changes during stressful situations. While this is generally not routinely done to assess your anxiety level, there is a type of treatment, known as biofeedback, which uses these kinds of measurement to help you learn to relax. Biofeedback will be discussed in greater detail in Chapter 5.

One application of biological measurement is the lie detector test, used in criminal investigations and sometimes by corporations to screen job applicants for honesty. The lie detector, or polygraph, does not measure emotion directly. Instead, it measures several physiological reactions that are associated with increases in your emotional responses. These include your breathing rate, your blood pressure, and perspiration. The presence of physical signs of an emotional reaction to questions about the alleged crime, while the individual is denying the act, is assumed to indicate lying and guilt. The lie detector test is not perfect, since the very nature of the questions can increase anxiety. For this reason, courts do not always accept lie detector test results as evidence.

Why is it difficult to measure anxiety? Are lie detector tests always accurate?

Psychological tests

Psychologists often use more sophisticated measures

of emotional adjustment and personality. The Rorschach test often involves the use of an inkblot or other unusual shape or design. If you are experiencing anxiety, you may see something frightening in an otherwise ordinary blot of ink or other design. Similarly, the Thematic Apperception Test (TAT) uses pictures and then asks you to create a story based on those pictures. The stories you create— the way you interpret those pictures—can help reveal whether or not you are experiencing anxiety.

As you can see, there are many different measurements of anxiety, and many different ways in which your anxiety level can be evaluated. These questions and measurement systems are a guide, but your own responses and feelings can also provide a useful guide. You know whether stress is helping or hurting you.

Psychologists use several different tests to measure anxiety. The Rorschach (or inkblot) test may reveal hidden fears. When viewing a series of ink patterns on paper, a person with anxiety disorder may say she sees something frightening.

Treating Anxiety

Abby was 12 years old, and she suffered from terrible migraine headaches. They always happened at night before a school day, never on Friday or Saturday nights and never over the summer. She went to a therapist for about nine months, and learned relaxation exercises. Systematic desensitization was used to help her deal with school-related anxiety. Her headaches disappeared and she ended her therapy. One month later, Abby's parents announced to the family that they are getting a divorce. Abby had sensed the tension between her parents but never mentioned it, and it contributed to her headaches.

The bad news is that so many of us suffer from anxiety and that it can affect our health and limit our happiness. The good news is that help is available. In most cases, you can learn to deal with anxiety, if not get rid of it entirely. This chapter discusses some of the many approaches to reducing anxiety. These approaches are sometimes called stress management. These include psychotherapy

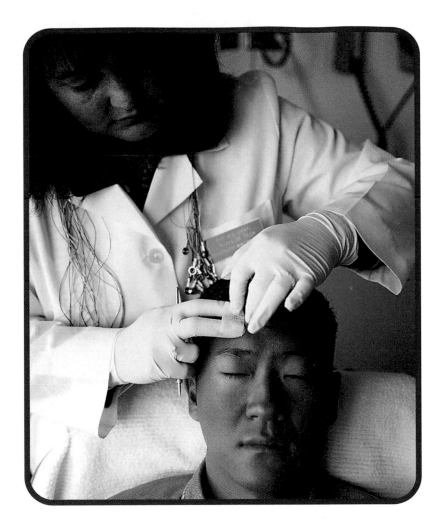

Treatments for anxiety vary. Psychotherapy can help you talk about your fears and learn to reduce them. Biofeedback can help you learn to make your body relax, even when faced with something frightening.

or counseling, biofeedback, and medication. There are also many coping strategies that you can use yourself.

Psychotherapy

For many years, psychotherapy was an intense approach that lasted many years. The psychotherapist would analyze your personality structure, defenses, and the earliest beginnings of your anxiety. The goal was to better understand your personality in order to be better able to control your emotions. In more recent years, alternative approaches to counseling and psychotherapy have been developed and proven to be effective. Some of these, called behavioral techniques, focus directly upon the anxiety itself, including your physical reactions, and have proven to be fast and effective ways to reduce stress. We cannot cover all of the approaches to therapy and counseling here, but we will highlight several methods that have been used to treat anxiety.

Some therapists use a combination of two techniques— muscle relaxation and something called **systematic desensitization**. Let's talk about muscle relaxation first. One of the signs of stress is muscle tension. You clench your teeth or your fists. The muscles of your head or neck get tense. You may experience a headache or stiff neck. We use the same word—TENSION—to mean physical and emotional tension. Muscles, like rubber bands, are elastic. But a rubber band stretches when it gets tense, while our muscles do the opposite—they contract. The contraction of muscles, which connect from one bone to another, accounts for the movement of parts of our body. Many years ago, a psychiatrist

Can you describe

how systematic desensitization may help you reduce anxiety?

reasoned that since anxiety involves muscle tension, teaching people to relax their muscles might help them reduce anxiety. He was right, and that method is still used today. Muscle relaxation training is a method for teaching a tense person to relax his or her body, one set of muscles at a time.

Now, let's look at systematic desensitization. This is a technique used to gradually help a tense or fearful person face the very situations or objects that make them anxious. How does it work? If you are afraid of heights, you might be asked to go up a ladder very slowly. The therapist monitors your emotional reaction. If you went up one step, you probably wouldn't get anxious, so you would be asked to take another step. During this process you are being helped to relax your muscles. As soon as you say that you are feeling even a tiny bit anxious, you come down from the ladder, practice more relaxation, and then try again. Gradually, in a procedure designed to make you feel safe and comfortable, you would make steady progress until you overcame the fear.

This process can be accomplished using imagined situations. People with high anxiety usually get stressed even thinking about a frightening situation or activity. A behavior therapist often helps you create a series of imaginary scenes—scenes in which you are actually doing whatever it is that frightens you. Once again, muscle relaxation is often used together with this technique. Little by little, the therapist will guide you through imagining the frightening scene, until you can imagine each step without fear. Once you can *imagine* yourself doing something that frightens you, you may find that you can actually do it without stress.

One criticism of this technique is that it doesn't actually help you understand why you are afraid. You are only taught to overcome the fear. This is a valid objection, but many people who find this technique helpful do not need to or want to know why they feel the fear—they only want to be able to master it.

Some therapists use a technique called **biofeedback** to make muscle relaxation easier. A machine that responds to electrical activity from muscle contractions is attached to various muscles in the body. The machine transforms the electrical impulse to a sound. The person trying to relax is able to hear when his muscles have relaxed so that he can better control the relaxation.

Many American therapists now use techniques called **Cognitive Behavior Therapy (or CBT)** to treat patients. CBT assumes that our emotions follow from our thoughts. We learn about our environment through experience but it is the way we interpret events that determines how we respond. Sometimes thoughts are not rational or logical. Yet if we have had those thoughts for a long time, we may not even notice them, or pay attention to whether or not they make sense. You

Does the way you think affect how you feel?

may find it difficult to take chances or face new challenges if you have grown up believing the message "I can't do it. I'm going to fail. I'm no good."

You can learn to stop these negative thoughts if you become aware of them. In CBT you learn to identify those thoughts and to re-examine them. You learn to begin to think differently about yourself and the world around you. You may begin to form healthier ideas, and to overcome the negative thoughts that have held you back. One technique, called **stress inoculation**, teaches you to practice certain anxiety-reducing thoughts to use during a stressful situation, such as a test or a time when you have to speak in front of a group of people. Stress inoculation is a powerful way that you can control your own anxiety.

An exciting new technique of therapy offers promise as a quick and efficient way to treat anxiety, phobias, nightmares, flashbacks, and other symptoms of post-traumatic stress disorder. Research and clinical practice with thousands of persons suffering these conditions suggests that Eye Movement Desensitization and Reprocessing (EMDR) can bring quick relief. The doctor who discovered this method of treatment used herself as her first patient. She was walking in the park when she began to be disturbed by a frightening thought. She began moving her eyes back and forth while thinking these thoughts. Suddenly, she realized that the thoughts were no longer disturbing to her. She spent the next 10 years perfecting and testing this eye movement technique, and EMDR is now practiced around the world. There is only one problem with this technique. We don't know why or how it works. Certainly more research is needed. EMDR offers great promise not only as a way of treating anxiety but also as a way to help us better understand how the mind works.

Some techniques don't require a therapist—you can do them yourself. Meditation is an ancient technique, first practiced in Far Eastern cultures. Meditation is a way of looking at yourself—not at what you would like yourself to be but what you actually are. This is not as easy as it sounds. Unfortunately, most of us seldom take a good look at what is going on in our minds. Meditation is somewhat similar to relaxation but is not directed specifically at any one fear. Yet meditation can help achieve a degree of calm and peace that relives anxiety, pain, and fear. It is a way of listening to yourself and by listening to better understand who lives inside your head. Sometimes there is more than one self inside you, and these selves are not always acting in harmony with each other. Meditation is a way of letting your thoughts flow wherever they might go, rather than directing them toward some problem. Meditation is not a difficult thing

Not all treatments for anxiety require a therapist. Meditation and yoga, techniques first practiced in the Far East, can help calm your thoughts and your body.

to learn. It can be as simple as finding a quiet place alone and listening to yourself breathe. One technique is to sit comfortably, close your eyes, count to five while you inhale and then count to 10 as you exhale. Listen to your thoughts as they follow one another. There are many resources that can teach you more about meditation. You will find one book (by Dale Carlson) listed at the end of this book. It can help with anxiety.

What else can you do to help reduce anxiety? Begin by taking a good look at your habits and lifestyle. Do you spend a lot of time alone, watching TV or on the computer? You may want to try exercising instead. Regular exercise (things like jogging, biking, swimming, dancing, and other sports) does more than just reduce anxiety—they can prevent it from starting. The regular use of muscle relaxation, meditation, and yoga exercises have been shown to reduce heart rate, blood pressure, muscle tension, respiration rate and other physical changes associated with anxiety.

As a last resort, some people need to receive medication that lowers their anxiety. Some of these medications may be used on an "as needed" basis; others must be taken regularly. These medications must be carefully monitored by a medically trained professional and, hopefully, used only for a short period of time.

Strengthening Families

■ Marie has been chosen for a starring role in the school play. She knows all of her lines, and she has been told that she has a real talent for acting. Marie desperately wants her parents to see her perform, but as the night of the play approaches, Marie becomes worried about her mother. Her mother has agoraphobia. She hasn't left her home in over two years. Each time she tries, she experiences severe panic. She has been seeing a therapist for months and also takes an anti-anxiety medication. But so far none of this has helped. Will she come to the school play?

Until now, we've talked about how anxiety affects us directly, as individuals. But that is only part of the story. Anxiety is contagious. It's not spread by a germ, like measles or chicken pox, but it spreads just the same and it impacts others in many ways. Anxiety in any family member affects everyone in the family. For this reason, therapists believe that treatment should involve all family members.

Anxiety doesn't only affect us as individuals—it affects those in our families as well. Family therapy can encourage supportive and caring behaviors that can reduce stress.

In the short stories at the beginning of each chapter have demonstrated, the symptoms of anxiety happen for a reason. Billy's fear of school is reinforced and supported by his mother, who has fears of her own. Without realizing what she is doing, she communicates to Billy that school is an unsafe place. She requires treatment as much as Billy does. He will not change unless she makes some drastic changes herself. Marie's mother's agoraphobia was causing problems for her entire family. Abby's headaches were based on more than school tension. As you can also see from these stories, anxiety does not affect only one member of the family, but can spread to, or even be encouraged by, other members of the family. For this reason, many therapists prefer to treat the entire family, not just one member, believing that one person may be expressing the stress of the entire family or that the anxiety may reflect a more general problem in the family.

What does family therapy involve? First, we need to understand what it means to have a "healthy family." Therapists and counselors agree that a healthy family is one in which members feel valued, supported, and safe. When that occurs, children in the family develop a healthy identity and learn the skills necessary to function in society. Members of a healthy family share, understand, and express feelings openly. They accept individual differences among family members. They develop a sense of caring. They cooperate with each other to accomplish chores and responsibilities. They can solve problems by working together—without fighting. They support each other in bad times. Having a healthy family doesn't mean that it is a family that never experiences sickness or other serious problems. But it does mean that when problems occur, the family can act together to find the answers they need.

How do you feel

when your parents listen to your problems, and show that they care about your feelings?

One of the main problems in unhealthy families is the inability to communicate with one another. Family members tend to ignore their feelings or to deny them because they are too dangerous, or too threatening. They are unable to admit when a bad situation exists. But if a

Communication is a key to successful family therapy. Learning to listen to those we love and showing them that they are important to us is a major step in treating anxiety.

problem is ignored, it doesn't disappear. It stays the same—or it gets worse. Unhealthy families tend to make each other feel worse. They may say one thing and mean another. Family therapists are skilled in helping families learn why they are unable to solve their own problems and to identify certain patterns or ways of behaving that may be hurting members of the family.

While there are many different ways to treat families, most family therapists would agree on certain general goals. First is to improve communication among all family members in an open and honest manner. Families must learn to "read" each other—to really listen and understand what each person is saying, and what they aren't saying. Second, the family must learn to solve their own problems. The family therapist provides a model for problem solving that the family learns to imitate. Third, the family must be honored and valued. Family members need to learn how important it is to keep their family whole and together, even if problems or separations occur. Finally, the family must also value each individual family member, respecting their differences and understanding the important role each member plays in the family as a whole. This means that each family member is entitled to his or her own feelings, ideas, needs, and attitudes. Each member should be honestly able to say, "I am a member of this family but I can also be my own person."

In the different approaches to family therapy, the focus is on different aspects of family life. In one approach, the family is seen as a complex system—a system that needs clear communication in order to work well. The goal of this approach is to make sure that all family members are communicating clearly, that signals are not misunderstood, and that no messages are ignored. In another approach, the therapy focuses on the structure of the family—the role each member plays, how power may shift from one family member to another, and how different family members band together in different situations. Yet another approach focuses on the family not

Can you describe the different approaches to family therapy, and how they help combat anxiety?

just as it exists today, but studies how family structures and ways of behaving can be passed from one generation to the next. In this approach, therapists explore a family's history, in the belief that problems did not simply spring up suddenly but may have occurred in a previous generation.

Preventing and coping

From reading this book, you should now understand that there are two major factors that determine whether or not you will develop anxiety and how well you will cope with it. The first is the influence of your thoughts, ideas, and attitudes upon your emotions. The second is the equally important impact of social factors, particularly the family. Families contribute to anxiety and also help to deal with it. Both factors—the influence of your thoughts and the influence of your family—determine whether the stressors in your life will result in stress and, in turn, will trigger anxiety disorders. It seems clear that the way to control anxiety is to develop healthy thoughts and to build healthy families.

Healthy thoughts

Much depends on how we interpret what happens to us. Having healthy thoughts means taking proper ownership for the good things that happen—seeing those positive outcomes realistically as the result of your own efforts. As much as possible, people need to experience a sense of control over what happens to them. That doesn't mean that everything can be controlled. But it does mean that it is important that you feel capable of improving your

How do you feel

when a difficult situation is beyond your control?

life, or making good things happen, of solving problems and taking charge of those stressors that can be controlled.

Fixing a problem may mean getting help from someone who is in a better position to fix it than you . . . or at least can help point you in the right direction.

Family support

There is little doubt that support available from family helps a person cope with stress. Families provide information, practical help, advice, and emotional support. If you have received emotional support from your family in the past, it is less likely that you will be overwhelmed by stressors. The problem is that people differ in the degree to which they can ask for, receive, and make use of family support. Of course, families also vary in their willingness or ability to provide support. But you need to be able to ask.

That's not as simple as it might seem. Parents who are ill or absent or emotionally limited may not be available for this support. We assume that most parents are well meaning and want to be there for you. But parents aren't perfect and sometimes are at a loss as to how to reach out to you. They get worried or scared or angry. They make mistakes, just as you do. They differ in the way they provide discipline and how they express affection.

Being a pre-teen and teenager can be difficult. You may become more distant from your parents. You may rebel. You may not like their rules. You may feel that you are grown up enough and mature enough to make your own rules. You may fight with your parents over what you wear, what time you go to bed, whether or not you will get an allowance—and how much it will be, what chores you are expected to do, your grades. . . . Your parents aren't quite ready to give up control. You may feel torn—torn between wanting and needing your parents and wanting to get as far away from them as possible. This is all normal—a part of growing up. It will take time and effort for your parents to

As we learn new ways to cope with life's stresses, we can begin to embrace the people, places, and things that anxiety once caused us to avoid—building healthy new relationships and attitudes for the future.

begin to recognize that you are growing up, but you need to be patient and act responsibly, to help smooth the way for a new relationship. Remember that a strong relationship with your parents will help you deal with problems—and control anxiety.

As you now understand, anxiety isn't simply an unpleasant feeling. Instead, it is a combination of thoughts, emotions, and physical changes. There isn't a single cause, and there isn't a single treatment. It doesn't simply exist in your head, or even in your body, but can be part of a much wider family and social context. It can move in to become a familiar and unwelcome guest, or it can be an occasional visitor whom you learn to send packing. It's up to you!

Glossary

Adrenalin — a chemical substance secreted by the adrenal gland that triggers responses like the fight or flight reaction.

Autonomic Nervous System — the part of the nervous system that controls that action of involuntary muscles like the heart, and involuntary actions like the secretion of substances from glands.

Anxiety — a vague, general sense of worry.

Biofeedback — a therapeutic technique that uses a machine to translate impulses from muscle contractions into sound, and helps the patient control anxiety by hearing when their muscles have relaxed.

Cognitive Behavior Therapy (CBT) — a therapeutic technique that assumes emotions are created by thoughts, and that a patient can control or change emotions by controlling or changing thoughts.

Conflict — a situation that creates anxiety because the outcome has the potential to be both positive and negative.

Defense mechanisms — strategies used to avoid or reduce anxiety.

Fight or flight reaction — a biological response to an emergency that prepares the body to fight a predator or flee a dangerous situation.

Interfering thoughts — thoughts that interfere with a person's ability to perform in a particular situation.

Parasympathetic nervous system — the part of the autonomic nervous system that controls the muscles of glands and internal organs.

Phobia — a severe form of anxiety provoked by a particular object or situation.

Glossary

Placebo — a substance that has no physical effects.

Somatic nervous system — the part of the nervous system that controls the action of voluntary muscles.

Stress inoculation — a therapeutic technique that teaches the patient to practice anxiety-reducing thoughts during stressful situations.

Stressor — a person, place, or event that creates anxiety.

Sympathetic nervous system — the part of the autonomic nervous system that controls responses like the fight or flight reaction.

Systematic desensitization — a technique used to help a tense or fearful person face the situations or objects that make them anxious.

Further Reading

Carlson, D. *Stop the pain: Teen meditations*. Madison, CT: Bick Publishing House, 1999.

Nadelson, C. C. *Uneasy lives: Understanding anxiety disorders*. Philadelphia, PA: Chelsea Publishing House, 2001.

Shapiro, F. Forrest, M. S. *EMDR : The breakthrough therapy for overcoming anxiety, stress, and trauma*. New York: Basic Books, 1997.

Index

About the Author

Marvin Rosen is a licensed clinical psychologist who practices in Media, Pennsylvania. He received his doctorate degree from the University of Pennsylvania in 1961. Since 1963, he has worked with intellectually and emotionally challenged people at Elwyn, Inc. in Pennsylvania, with clinical, administrative, research, and training responsibilities. He also conducts a private practice of psychology. Dr. Rosen has taught psychology at the University of Pennsylvania, Bryn Mawr College, and West Chester University. He has written or edited seven book and numerous professional articles in the areas of psychology, rehabilitation, emotional disturbance, and mental retardation.